Richard Molloy

THE SEPARATION

OBERON BOOKS
LONDON

WWW.OBERONBOOKS.COM

First published in 2015 by Oberon Books Ltd
521 Caledonian Road, London N7 9RH
Tel: +44 (0) 20 7607 3637 / Fax: +44 (0) 20 7607 3629
e-mail: info@oberonbooks.com
www.oberonbooks.com

A catalogue record for this book is available from the British
Library.

PB ISBN: 978-1-78319-858-0
E ISBN: 978-1-78319-859-7

Cover design by Issa James

Visit www.oberonbooks.com to read more about all our books
and to buy them. You will also find features, author interviews and
news of any author events, and you can sign up for e-newsletters
so that you're always first to hear about our new releases.

For (not about) Mary and Philip

The Separation was first performed at Project Arts Centre in Dublin on 4 June 2014, with the following cast:

STEPHEN HANRAHAN	David Murray
MARION HANRAHAN	Carrie Crowley
GERTY HANRAHAN	Roxanna Nic Liam
MOLLY MACDONALD	Susan Stanley

Creative Team

Director	Simon Evans
Designer	Amy Cook
Lighting Designer	Zia Holly
Music & Sound	Ed Lewis
Production Manager	Eoin Kilkenny
Stage Manager	Suzie Foster
Producers	Susan Stanley & Richard Molloy

The production then transferred to Theatre503 on 30 January 2015, with the following changes to cast and crew:

STEPHEN HANRAHAN	Owen McDonnell
Lighting Designer	Will Evans
Associate Director	Emma Butler
Production Manager	James Turner Inman

Characters

STEPHEN HANRAHAN
a journalist, mid-forties.

MARION HANRAHAN
his wife, a social worker, mid-forties.

GERTY HANRAHAN
their daughter, sixteen.

MOLLY MACDONALD
a colleague of Stephen's, Irish-American, late twenties.

Setting and Time

The play is set over a single weekend in June 1995:

Scene One, Friday night.

Scene Two, Saturday morning.

Scenes Three and *Four*, Saturday afternoon.

Scene Five, Sunday midday.

The action takes place in Dun Laoghaire, a predominantly middle-class seaside town in the south-Dublin suburbs.

SCENE ONE

The living room of a large house in Dun Laoghaire in south Dublin.

There is one window, looking out on a large back garden (though this need not be visible), and two doorways, one of which gives access to the hallway and the front door of the house and the other to the upstairs and the rest of the house.

The living room is untidy. There are shelves overflowing with books, CDs, vinyl, cassette tapes, video tapes. A stereo system with disorderly piles of CDs beside it. Video cases on the floor by the television. Stacks of newspapers, some so old they are discoloured. A well-stocked drinks cabinet. A coffee table beneath which, and perhaps upon which, there are more newspapers. A couch and armchair, once fairly tasteful and expensive, now in less than immaculate condition. On the mantelpiece above the fireplace, a clock, and a picture frame with a photo of a baby girl. Above the mantelpiece, a mirror.

The room is in darkness.

We hear heavy rain outside…the sound of a phone ringing, off, then the phone stops. Shortly afterwards, the sound of the front door opening, off. A light in the hallway, commotion, off.

The living-room door opens. The lights go on.

STEPHEN: *(Off.)* Go on. Get in.

> *MOLLY bundles in followed by STEPHEN.*
>
> *They are both drenched.*
>
> *They stand, looking at one another for a moment.*
>
> *They laugh. She drops her handbag on the couch.*

MOLLY: *(Looking herself over, half-laughing, half-lamenting.)* Oww.

STEPHEN: *(Referring to the rain.)* That's biblical, that is.

> *She's too caught up in feeling wet to respond.*

STEPHEN: I should get you some clothes or –

MOLLY: Have you got a hairdryer?

STEPHEN: Ehm…a towel?

MOLLY: That'll do.

STEPHEN: I'll be right back.

He leaves.

She stays rooted to the same spot, as though moving would worsen her plight.

She turns her head to look around the room. A moment passes.

He throws her a towel from the doorway.

STEPHEN: Towel. Back in a sec.

She catches the towel.

MOLLY: Thanks.

She dries her hair, moves to the mirror, examines herself.

MOLLY: Oh my God.

She attempts for a moment to sort herself out, then notices the photo on the mantelpiece, picks it up. When she hears STEPHEN returning, she puts the picture down, moves away from the mantelpiece and continues to dry her hair.

STEPHEN comes in. He has changed clothes. He is carrying a Bryan Adams t-shirt and a pair of old, unfashionable tracksuit bottoms (perhaps made by O'Neill's.).

STEPHEN: *(Giving them to her.)* T-shirt. Trousers.

She is unimpressed.

MOLLY: I can't…This is…

STEPHEN: What?

MOLLY: Bryan Adams.

STEPHEN: *(Feigning puzzlement, but enjoying the situation.)* Yeah. All I could find. It's not even mine. I don't know where it came from.

She looks at him sceptically.

STEPHEN: Seriously. Look at my CDs. I'm fuckin' cool. I wouldn't condone Bryan Adams.

Short pause.

STEPHEN: Well, *Summer of '69* obviously / but –

MOLLY: You expect me to sit here in some pissy old sweatpants –

STEPHEN: Ah here, there's no need for that –

MOLLY: And a Bryan Adams t-shirt.

STEPHEN: I could look for something else.

Short pause.

STEPHEN: I think I have a Meat Loaf t-shirt somewhere.

MOLLY: *(Good-natured.)* Oh fuck off.

They laugh a little, then fall into an awkward deadlock. They look at one another silently for a moment. Neither one knows what to do next. Each expects the other to act.

STEPHEN: Well.

MOLLY: Yeah.

Short pause.

MOLLY: I, uh, I need to change so…

STEPHEN: Oh, okay. Eh, should I *(Points to the door.)* …or –

MOLLY: Could I –

STEPHEN: You could go to the bedroom…or the bathroom –

MOLLY: Yeah, could I? The bathroom.

STEPHEN: Sure yeah, yeah.

Short pause.

MOLLY: Um, where is it?

STEPHEN: Oh okay –

MOLLY: Are you doing this on purpose?

STEPHEN: Doing what? No. It's eh…Follow the stairs right to the top. Can't miss it.

MOLLY: Okay… *(In a Terminator voice.)* 'I'll be back.'

She goes to leave then remembers her handbag, comes back for it, smiles…

MOLLY: Uh yeah, I'll…

She leaves.

STEPHEN: *(As she's going.)* There's a pair of slippers there by the sink if you want to borrow them.

MOLLY: *(Off, light-hearted.)* I probably don't. But I might bring them down so you can use them to go fuck yourself.

He laughs gently then –

STEPHEN: That was rude.

He waits a moment until he is sure that she has gone upstairs then rushes to the drinks cabinet. He opens a bottle of whiskey, but does not take a drink – rather he inhales it, which evokes in him a powerful mixture of pleasure and torment. He puts the lid back on, returns the bottle to the cabinet.

He goes to the book shelves, takes a book, stands there pretending to be engrossed in the book, attempting to look sophisticated, then realises –

STEPHEN: Wine.

He hurries back to the drinks cabinet, takes a single wine glass and a bottle of wine, sets them on the coffee table, goes back to the drinks cabinet, finds a bottle opener, opens the bottle with difficulty, and pours some wine into the glass.

For a moment he is still, thinking.

STEPHEN: Fuck it.

He returns to the drinks cabinet, opens the whiskey again, takes a swig from the bottle. And another swig. And another.

He puts the bottle back in the cabinet, then fishes in his pocket for an unwrapped mint. He blows the lint off it and puts it in his mouth.

He moves to the couch and arranges himself on it in what is supposed to be a sexy position, perhaps fixes his crotch. He waits. When he hears MOLLY coming back down the stairs, he removes the mint from his mouth, disposes of it behind the couch. As he does so, the door opens dramatically. MOLLY stands in the doorway like a cowboy about to enter a saloon, only she's wearing the t-shirt and tracksuit bottoms, both of which are too big for her, and a pair of furry, oversize novelty slippers.

STEPHEN: Oh. Hi.

He tries not to laugh.

STEPHEN: You look…ravishing.

MOLLY: Ha. Ha. Ha.

STEPHEN: Honestly.

MOLLY: I can't quite believe this, Stephen –

STEPHEN: Well, I'm rather cheesed off too. 'Cause the wardrobe of women's clothes I'd had prepared for this exact eventuality, wouldn't you know it? It's out on loan. To Kylie. Or Madonna. I forget which.

MOLLY: Mmm, is it?

STEPHEN: A case of unfortunate timing is all. But sure you might as well come in and sit down anyway.

MOLLY: I might as well.

She doesn't move.

STEPHEN: Eh –

MOLLY: There's something I've wanted to say to you all evening.

Short pause.

STEPHEN: Okay. Sounds serious.

MOLLY: It is. It's kind of a secret.

STEPHEN: Right, eh, are you going to stand out there or –

MOLLY: I'm worried you'll ask me to leave.

STEPHEN: Hah? Would you don't be ridiculous? Come in and sit down. Look it, there's a glass of wine there for you.

She enters the room and sits down beside him, leaving her handbag next to the couch.

MOLLY: Are you not having one?

STEPHEN: No. I told you. I haven't touched a drop in months, Molly. But you go on –

MOLLY: Thanks. I might have some in a minute –

STEPHEN: Do you know what they call someone who doesn't drink, by the way, the Irish?

MOLLY: Uh, no –

STEPHEN: A *pioneer*. Isn't that gas? A pioneer. Like you're discovering a new continent or something. *(Shouting, in an exaggerated Irish accent.)* 'Jays boys, I'm going to sail the fuckin' ocean to the uncharted lands of sobriety.'

MOLLY: Stephen, can I –

STEPHEN: Oh, sorry. Sorry. Eh, go ahead.

MOLLY: Uhm, okay. Do you promise you won't get angry?

STEPHEN: O' course –

MOLLY: 'Cause it's kinda big –

STEPHEN: *(Gentle.)* Molly. I promise.

She smiles.

MOLLY: Uhm, so…I've been offered a job. At the *Times*.

STEPHEN: I know.

MOLLY: Excuse me?

STEPHEN: I know.

MOLLY: What do you mean you know?

STEPHEN: They offered me a job too.

MOLLY: *(Shocked.)* What?

STEPHEN: Well, it's been going on for nearly a year actually. They wanted to bring me in as news editor last…October, I think it was, but it, I don't know, there was some fuckin' union complication 'cause they were letting some other people go at the same time, or…Anyway it's all sorted now. I've accepted the offer. I'm defecting in September. But the thing is I told them I wanted you to come with me.

Short pause.

MOLLY: You told them?

STEPHEN: Yes.

MOLLY: *(Disappointed.)* I see.

STEPHEN: Eh –

MOLLY: Right. Way to shit on my sense of achievement, Mr Hanrahan.

STEPHEN: Hah? Ah no. C'mon out of that –

MOLLY: I'm one of your *terms and conditions* –

STEPHEN: No. What? No. That's not it at all. They're excited about you, Molly.

MOLLY: Are they?

STEPHEN: Yes. Completely fuckin' love you, so they do.

MOLLY: Really?

STEPHEN: Seriously. Had their eye on you for ages. When I suggested it, they were like, *(In an American accent.)* 'Sign me the fuck up.'

MOLLY: *(Pleased with herself.)* Really?

STEPHEN: Yeah. Absolutely.

MOLLY: Oh.

Short pause.

MOLLY: Sorry. I didn't mean to sound ungrateful.

STEPHEN: Ah no. Do you think you'll accept it?

MOLLY: Uhm, I *want* to –

STEPHEN: You should –

MOLLY: No, I know. I just, I feel bad, you know, about the Indo –

STEPHEN: Are you mad? Sure, that fuckin' arse-rag's been 'round for donkey's years. It'll survive without the two of us.

MOLLY: Yeah. Maybe –

STEPHEN: The thing is…and, you know, this is important…

Short pause.

MOLLY: Yeah?

STEPHEN: 'There ain't no use in complainin' *(Sings, from 'Summer of '69'.)* when you got a job to do.'

He finds this very funny.

MOLLY: *(Smiling.)* Shut up.

Short pause.

MOLLY: So you're my fairy godmother then?

STEPHEN: Yeah.

They smile.

STEPHEN: Would you like to see my magic wand?

He laughs again, delighted with himself. She's stone-faced. He dead-stops.

STEPHEN: Sorry.

Short pause.

MOLLY: What's going on here, Stephen?

STEPHEN: What do you mean?

MOLLY: You and me.

STEPHEN: I don't know.

MOLLY: It's been kind of a long time since –

STEPHEN: I know…I'm sorry. It wasn't like…I didn't mean to ignore it –

MOLLY: No, I know. Neither did I –

STEPHEN: Just, there was a lot going on, you know, I couldn't –

MOLLY: I'm not saying I expected you to, I don't know…It's just, it was weird, we never really…acknowledged it, or –

STEPHEN: I know –

MOLLY: But it seemed like it was more than just a one-off thing.

STEPHEN: Yeah.

Awkward pause.

MOLLY: Your house is lovely.

STEPHEN: Thank you.

MOLLY: Not really how I imagined it though.

STEPHEN: No?

MOLLY: No. It's uh, it's messier.

STEPHEN: *(Sarcastically.)* Oho you're very funny. *(Seriously but with a little mischief.)* You imagined my house though, did you?

MOLLY: Yes, actually.

STEPHEN: Did you imagine being *in* my house?

MOLLY: Yeah. I did –

STEPHEN: What did you see when you imagined being in my house?

MOLLY: Oh you know: You. Me. Oversize novelty slippers.

STEPHEN: Oh yeah? Were we eh…Were we kissing, by any chance?

MOLLY: Excuse me?

STEPHEN: 'Cause if *I* imagined you in my house I think that's what we'd be doing. We'd be kissing.

MOLLY: Would we?

STEPHEN: Yes. *If* I imagined you in my house.

MOLLY: Well, I'm sorry to disappoint you.

STEPHEN: Oh –

MOLLY: You're gonna have to do a little better than that?

STEPHEN: Am I?

MOLLY: Yes. I mean, you'll have to forgive me here, Stephen, but in light of what's gone before, i.e., your failure to even acknowledge our little rendezvous at the Christmas party, I might take a bit more…cajoling.

STEPHEN: Right. I see… Cajoling.

MOLLY: Yes.

STEPHEN: I thought I had been cajoling you for weeks –

MOLLY: What?

STEPHEN: The lads in the office were saying to me, 'Jays Stephen, that's some fine fuckin' cajoling you're doing there on that Molly one. She'll be eating outta your hand, so she will, in no time.'

MOLLY: 'That Molly one'? You had better be kidding me.

STEPHEN: We were thinking of running a front page story: MASTER CAJOLER, STEPHEN HANRAHAN, IN ACTION AT THE INDEPENDENT.

MOLLY: Once again, ha di fucking ha.

STEPHEN: Alongside MOLLY MACDONALD, TRAITOR, JOINS TIMES.

MOLLY: Oh now that's…You're going backwards at the moment, just so you know.

STEPHEN: Am I?

MOLLY: You're getting further away from that kiss.

STEPHEN: Ah no.

MOLLY: It's a small dot on the horizon.

STEPHEN: Well I better –

MOLLY: About to disappear.

STEPHEN: Here eh…

He looks at her.

STEPHEN: I think there's eh…You've got something…

He gestures toward one of his own eyes.

MOLLY: What?

STEPHEN: You've got something in your eye there.

MOLLY: Oh. Uhm…Really…?

She goes to stand up to look in the mirror but…

STEPHEN: No, hang on, c'm'ere.

She stays seated.

STEPHEN: Let me eh…

MOLLY: Which eye?

STEPHEN: This one…Just eh –

MOLLY: Can you –

STEPHEN: Lean your head back there…Sorry.

MOLLY: I don't feel anything. Can you see something?

STEPHEN: Yeah…

MOLLY: Well, can you…What is it?

STEPHEN: It's hard to –

MOLLY: Let me see.

She goes to the mirror.

MOLLY: This one?

STEPHEN: *(Agreeing.)* Mmmm –

MOLLY: There's nothing there, Stephen. What are you –

STEPHEN: There is. C'm'ere.

MOLLY: *(Still looking.)* There's not.

STEPHEN: *(Gesturing for her to come back.)* Just…

She sits down again. He looks in her eye.

STEPHEN: Yeah. I can see it.

MOLLY: What? What are you –

STEPHEN: Jesus.

MOLLY: What do you mean 'Jesus'? What is it?

STEPHEN: Wow.

MOLLY: Wow what? You're starting to freak me out.

STEPHEN: Molly, I don't know how to break this to you, but –

MOLLY: What? Would you –

STEPHEN: There's a little man inside your eye.

Short pause while she realises she's been had.

MOLLY: *(Slapping his arm.)* You fucking prick, you had me
worried there for a minute.

STEPHEN: Stop it. Stop it. I'm serious. I'd heard about this, Molly, but I never thought it was true.

MOLLY: What the hell are you talking about?

STEPHEN: *(Gesturing to one of her eyes.)* There's a man, a little fella, lives in this eye here.

MOLLY: *(Starting to smile about it.)* Oh really?

STEPHEN: Yes. A writer, in fact. Lives in here with his little typewriter. Types out messages all day long. You never see him?

MOLLY: No. Oddly enough –

STEPHEN: Ah that's shocking. You should keep an eye out for him. Hang on a second. He's typing something now.

MOLLY: He is, is he?

STEPHEN: Something important probably.

MOLLY: What's it say?

STEPHEN: Difficult to see. The writing's very small. Just tilt your head a little to the… M-O-L Molly… Molly something… Molly…What's the second word? Molly… *(Emphatically.)* Molly smells.

MOLLY: *(Slapping him again, laughing.)* You fucker –

STEPHEN: Hey –

MOLLY: You call this cajoling?

STEPHEN: Don't shoot the messenger. I'm only telling you what the little man in your eye says.

MOLLY: Very funny.

STEPHEN: *(Still looking into her eye.)* Would you look! He's typing something else here.

MOLLY: Just be careful you.

STEPHEN: Hold it there now 'til I have a look…Ah it's very difficult to read. Only the finest, you know. You have to have a certain skill… *(Pretending to read.)*… M-O… Molly…must…kiss…a…hand…some, handsome…man…

It's…the…only…way…to…all-e-viate *(Breaks off reading for a second.)* 'Alleviate', Jaysis… *(Pretending to read again.)* the…terrible…stench.

She slaps him again.

MOLLY: You're ridiculous.

STEPHEN: He's a bit rude, isn't he? Although he does have an extensive vocabulary for a man trapped inside a woman's eye.

MOLLY: Totally ridiculous. Do you know any handsome men?

Short pause.

STEPHEN: Ehm.

MOLLY: What?

STEPHEN: You're sitting beside one.

Short pause. She considers this.

MOLLY: Naw.

STEPHEN: *(Sings, from Bryan Adams 'Everything I Do…'.)* 'You know it's true.'

She laughs.

MOLLY: I'm not so sure.

STEPHEN: C'mon.

MOLLY: I suppose, if we're being generous, you might just qualify.

STEPHEN: 'Course I qualify.

MOLLY: *(Edging closer to him.)* We could give it a try.

STEPHEN: I think we should.

MOLLY: To alleviate the terrible stench.

STEPHEN: Exactly…

She laughs gently. They stare at one another for a moment, then they kiss, tentatively at first, but with growing passion. He breaks off –

STEPHEN: Cajoling, see?

She smiles. They kiss again but are interrupted by the sound of the phone, off. MOLLY pulls away. They stare at one another.

MOLLY: Hi.

STEPHEN: Hi.

MOLLY: You wanna get that?

STEPHEN: Nah, the machine'll…

The ringing stops.

STEPHEN: There you go.

They stare at one another.

MOLLY: You looking for the little man again?

STEPHEN: Nah. He's gone.

MOLLY: Oh.

STEPHEN: Packed up for the day.

MOLLY: Home to the wife and kids.

They kiss again.

STEPHEN: Should we *(Unsaid: 'go upstairs?'.)*…

She nods her head.

He gets up. She doesn't move.

STEPHEN: What's wrong?

MOLLY: Nothing. I just, I don't want this to be –

STEPHEN: It's not.

MOLLY: Back in the office on Monday like nothing happened. *(In what is meant to be his voice.)* 'Gimme ten pars on the mad cow disease. What was your name?'

STEPHEN: *(Smiling.)* That's not…I don't sound like that, by the way, but *(With gravity.)* I'm not treating this lightly, Molly. I know the last time…The circumstances…

MOLLY: What circumstances?

Short pause.

STEPHEN: Let's not ruin this…

Pause. She looks at him intently, trying to read him.

MOLLY: Promise me then –

STEPHEN: I promise.

They stare at one another.

STEPHEN: I promise.

He kisses her.

STEPHEN: C'mon.

She gets up. He smiles, takes her hand.

STEPHEN: *(Sings as they exit, again from 'Summer of '69'.)* 'Oh and when you held my hand, I knew that it was now or never.'

MOLLY: *(Exiting, or off.)* Would you stop with the fucking Bryan Adams already?

He continues singing as they climb the stairs. His voice becomes more distant and dies out. It is replaced by the sound of the phone ringing and eventually the answering machine message.

STEPHEN: Hi, this is Stephen. Leave a message and your name will be entered into a hat. From the ensuing lottery, a select number of calls will be returned.

A beep.

MARION: Stephen, it's Marion, do you not answer your fucking phone? It's like trying to contact the bloody Pope. Listen, Gerty and I had a row earlier. She stormed out of the house. I don't know where she is. Can you call me, Stephen, please? Call me, you useless bag of shite. *(Hangs up.)*

Silence.

Lights out.

SCENE TWO

The following morning about eleven o'clock. It's still raining outside. A rather unimpressive breakfast is laid out on the coffee table.

MOLLY enters in her knickers and the Bryan Adams t-shirt, humming or whistling the tune to 'Everything I Do (I Do It For You.)', occasionally voicing some of the lyrics. She has a little snoop around the room, perhaps eats some toast or drinks some coffee or orange juice until she hears a noise in the hallway – the sound of the newspaper being delivered – and goes out to investigate.

STEPHEN, in his dressing gown, enters from the other door, humming 'Everything I Do'. When MOLLY returns he greets her with –

STEPHEN: *(Sings, removes his dressing gown as he does so.)*
'Baaaaybeeee I'm hot just like an oven.'

Now wearing only a pair of less than immaculate Y-fronts, he presents himself to her.

MOLLY looks at him askew.

STEPHEN: What?

MOLLY: Nothing.

STEPHEN: What?

She considers pointing at, and commenting on, his underpants, but she stops herself.

MOLLY: Nothing. Nothing. At. All.

She turns her attention to the newspaper. He struts over to the window and looks at the rain.

STEPHEN: *(In a silly voice.)* And if you looked closely, you could just about see the animals lining up two-by-two.

He stays there a moment.

MOLLY: Did you hear the news?

STEPHEN: Hah?

MOLLY: It's in all the papers this morning.

He turns to face her.

STEPHEN: What're you talking about?

MOLLY: Well, apparently, Irish men have discovered…
foreplay.

STEPHEN: *(Gently dismissive.)* Ah shut up.

MOLLY: No it's true. Irish men – just, uh, yesterday – they
discovered foreplay.

STEPHEN: Is that right –

MOLLY: *(Shouts, in the most unsophisticated Irish accent possible.)*
'Brace yourself missus, I'm coming in.'

STEPHEN: *(Moving toward her.)* Ah, you're very funny. And also
a little bit racist.

MOLLY: My dad's Irish. I can say whatever the hell I like
about Irish men.

He kisses her.

STEPHEN: Racist and sexist.

He kisses her again.

STEPHEN: I know about foreplay.

He removes her t-shirt.

STEPHEN: I'm the St. Patrick of foreplay. I brought it to the
Irish people.

She lies back on the couch.

STEPHEN: And then I drove out the imperialist American
snakes.

He climbs on top of her.

MOLLY: Hang on, Stephen.

Short pause.

STEPHEN: Are you alright?

MOLLY: Yes…I'm happy we're doing this.

STEPHEN: So am I.

MOLLY: I don't mean this *(Meaning 'sex'.)* …I mean –

STEPHEN: I know what you mean.

MOLLY: Do you?

STEPHEN: Yes.

MOLLY: I'd like it to work out this time.

STEPHEN: Me too.

MOLLY: It's just, if I take the job, if we're working together, I wouldn't want there to be any…problem, you know, between you and me.

STEPHEN: Why would there be a problem, sure?

MOLLY: I don't know, like, if something went wrong between us, if we –

STEPHEN: Ah but you can't let that influence your decision –

MOLLY: No, I know. You're right –

STEPHEN: Are you gonna take it then?

Short pause.

MOLLY: I think so. I mean, I don't know –

STEPHEN: Ah that's brilliant –

MOLLY: I'm not saying for sure, but I should, shouldn't I?

STEPHEN: Of course, you should –

MOLLY: I just, I wish you hadn't told me –

STEPHEN: I know. I'm sorry –

MOLLY: But it's too good an opportunity to turn down, isn't it?

STEPHEN: Yes. Ah that's great news. Let's celebrate…

He kisses her, and they begin – just for a moment – to lose themselves in one another, but there's a knock on the front door of the house, off. They stop kissing. A pause.

MOLLY: Did you hear something?

STEPHEN: Was there a knock?

They listen.

We hear the front door of the house opening…closing.

MOLLY: There's someone coming in.

STEPHEN: How could there be?

Footsteps in the hallway.

MOLLY: Get up, would you?

MARION is suddenly standing in the doorway, holding an umbrella.

MARION: Stephen.

MOLLY: *(Overlapping.)* Oh my God.

STEPHEN: *(Jumping up off MOLLY, overlapping.)* Sweet suffering mother of almighty fuck.

MOLLY scrambles into the t-shirt again.

MARION: What the fuck is going on?

STEPHEN: What do you mean what the fuck is going on?

MARION: Is Gerty here?

STEPHEN: What?

MARION: Gerty. Your daughter.

STEPHEN: I know who she is –

MARION: Is she here?

STEPHEN: Is she – It wouldn't fuckin' appear so, would it?

MOLLY: *(Going to leave.)* I uh… I have to get some clothes.

MARION: *(Offering her hand.)* Hello, love. I'm Marion, Stephen's wife.

MOLLY doesn't know what to do.

STEPHEN: *Ex*-wife.

MARION: We're still married in the eyes of God, Stephen. And, in fact, in the eyes of the law. *(To MOLLY.)* Is that my t-shirt you're wearing, pet?

MOLLY is dumbfounded.

MARION: If you like, you could use my umbrella…to cover your modesty.

MOLLY: I uh… Excuse me.

She bundles out of the room.

MARION: She's lovely.

STEPHEN: What the hell are you doing?

MARION: Gerty said she was due here today.

STEPHEN: At two. It's *(Looking at the clock on the mantelpiece.)*…
eleven. Why the fuck are you here?

MARION: She's missing, Stephen. I called you several times –
(Continues.)

STEPHEN: *(Overlapping.)* Whoa, whoa, hang on –

MARION: – I left a message –

STEPHEN: Would you hang on, Marion…? What do you mean
she's missing?

She sighs.

MARION: We had a row yesterday. She stormed out. I haven't
seen her since. Do you not check your fuckin' –

STEPHEN: Since when?

MARION: What?

STEPHEN: You haven't seen her since when?

MARION: Since we had the row.

STEPHEN: Which was when?

MARION: Yesterday. About six.

STEPHEN: Right. Fuck. And you've called her friends?

MARION: *(Sarcastic.)* No, Stephen, I haven't called anyone.
(Suddenly sincere again, biting.) Of course, I've called her
fuckin' friends –

STEPHEN: I'm only asking –

MARION: No one's heard anything.

STEPHEN: Jesus.

He sighs.

STEPHEN: Does she have a fella or something we don't know
about?

MARION: No. I don't think so. I thought she might be here.

STEPHEN: No eh…I haven't heard from her since…Monday, I think it was, we arranged –

MARION: You arranged to see her without informing me.

STEPHEN: What? Oh I'm sorry. I need your permission now to see my own daughter, is that it?

MARION: No, that's not it, Stephen. You don't need my permission, but given the circumstances –

STEPHEN: I thought you'd be fuckin' pleased, Marion, after…

MARION: Yeah, 'after', Stephen…'after'…There's a big fuckin' 'after', isn't there? But we won't go into that –

STEPHEN: Alright, just…What was the…The row, what was it about?

MARION: It was a row, okay. You don't need to concern yourself with it. Just call me as soon as she gets here, will you? If she gets here.

STEPHEN: You're going?

MARION: No, I'm gonna stick around. I thought you, me and your little naked friend could play a few rounds of the Trivial Pursuit.

She goes to leave.

STEPHEN: Marion…

She puts her head back in the door.

STEPHEN: She'll show up…Don't worry.

She briefly considers making a conciliatory response but instead…

MARION: Your underpants are a holy fuckin' disgrace.

We hear her going out and the front door closing, off.

STEPHEN: Right.

He is still momentarily, pondering the whole situation, wondering what to do.

STEPHEN: Fuck.

He puts his dressing gown on.

STEPHEN: Fuck. Fuck. Fuck…

He goes to the drinks cabinet, opens the whiskey, swigs from the bottle.

We hear MOLLY coming down the stairs. He quickly puts the bottle away – perhaps spilling whiskey on himself and just about managing to clean himself up – before she arrives. She walks into the room purposefully, wearing the clothes she had on when she arrived at the house yesterday. She searches for something.

STEPHEN: Jays, the old antenna let me down there. Didn't see that one coming…What're you doing?

MOLLY: *(Without looking at him.)* Have you seen my purse?

STEPHEN: Hah?

MOLLY: My handbag.

STEPHEN: Is something the matter?

MOLLY: I'm leaving, Stephen. That's what the matter is.

STEPHEN: Ah Molly, there's no need for that.

MOLLY: There's a very big fucking need.

STEPHEN: Look, I can see that was a bit awkward.

MOLLY: *(Abruptly stops searching, faces him.)* Are you fucking psychotic, Stephen? That wasn't 'a bit awkward'. That was one of the most humiliating experiences of my life. *(Incredulous.)* Your wife – your fucking *wife* – *(Continues.)*

STEPHEN: *(Overlapping.)* She's my *ex*-wife –

MOLLY: – arrives out of fucking nowhere. Like a, like a fucking magician, Stephen. Alaka-fucking-zam. I'm sprawled out naked on *her* couch with *her* naked fucking husband on top of me.

STEPHEN: It's not her couch. She doesn't live here anymore.

MOLLY: Oh, excuse me, Mrs Hanrahan. You mean you're married to this man? Oh, he seems to have misplaced his penis in my vagina. How careless of him.

STEPHEN: Listen, you're totally overreacting here.

MOLLY: *(Overreacting.)* Don't tell me I'm overreacting. *(Searching again.)* I mean the t-shirt, Stephen. What the fuck? You gave your wife's t-shirt to me to wear. How do you explain that one?

STEPHEN: She's not my wife, I keep telling you –

MOLLY: 'Cause that's just –

STEPHEN: She's my *ex*-wife –

MOLLY: That's a bit fucking creepy, actually, if you don't mind me saying so.

STEPHEN: It's only a t-shirt. You're making a big deal out of nothing.

MOLLY: It's my own fat fucking fault. I should have listened.

STEPHEN: Listened? For the front door like?

MOLLY: *(Finds handbag.)* No, not for the front door. To my own better instinct and to the droves of people who warned me to stay the fuck away from you.

STEPHEN: Who fuckin' –

MOLLY: It doesn't matter, does it? The fucking stupid thing is I fell for it all there for a minute – the little man in my eye and the job and all your bullshit.

STEPHEN: The job's not bullshit.

MOLLY: I thought we could –

STEPHEN: We can, Molly.

MOLLY: No, Stephen. I'm going.

STEPHEN: So, what, so that's it – it's just, it's over – just like that…?

She goes to leave.

STEPHEN: Molly, hang on, would you…Listen to me for a sec – *(He raises his voice.)* Would you stop? *(She stops. He lowers his voice again.)* Please. Just let me, even if you're gonna leave, just let me say something…

Pause.

STEPHEN: Look at me.

She does.

STEPHEN: Thank you. Please just let me say this and then if you want to go, you can...

Short pause. He struggles with what he's going to say.

STEPHEN: She's my ex-wife. We separated in December, okay? Six months ago. This is not her house. She doesn't live here anymore, I swear to you. She...I had to move out for a couple of months until she found somewhere, and then I moved back in after. She hasn't lived here since then, since March. She must still have a key though. That's how she...I had no idea she was going to show up like that. The thing is my daughter went missing last night and...I'm not fuckin' proud of this but I haven't seen her since it all happened, since the separation, which was Christmas. But we arranged...She's supposed to be coming here later on today. That's the reason...Marion thought she might be here already, do you see? And that's why the phone last night –

MOLLY: Which if you had answered, like I suggested, we wouldn't've had this this morning.

STEPHEN: Ah Molly, c'mon. I'm saying sorry here. I didn't mean to embarrass you. I had no idea...I'm sorry, Molly. There's nothing sinister...It's just...

A long pause.

MOLLY: What's happened your daughter? She's missing?

STEPHEN: Yeah... Well...

MOLLY: What?

STEPHEN: Ah, I don't know.

MOLLY: Is she missing or not, Stephen?

STEPHEN: No. Yes. Just...There was a night last December. Her mother and I were having a row. She went off, didn't come back 'til the next night, so...

MOLLY: You think maybe she's just –

STEPHEN: Yeah. She'll come back.

MOLLY: But you haven't seen her anyway, since –

STEPHEN: No.

Something clicks in MOLLY's head.

MOLLY: Hang on, December…?

STEPHEN: What?

MOLLY: It was December? The separation?

STEPHEN: Yes.

MOLLY: Before or after…?

STEPHEN: Hah?

MOLLY: Before or after we…You and I –

STEPHEN: After but –

MOLLY: So, what, your wife left because of me?

STEPHEN: No. No –

MOLLY: Jesus Christ –

STEPHEN: No, Molly, would you listen? It was nothing to do with that. Sure she was – She had her own fuckin'…

MOLLY: What…?

STEPHEN: You know…

Short pause.

MOLLY: She cheated on you?

STEPHEN: Yes. I think…but that's not…Look, I swear to you, you had nothing to do with it. It was well over by then and I never even told her about the…about what happened. Nobody knows. In the office even. At least not from me. Jesus, I haven't told anyone about the separation. The only reason I'm telling you now is…I thought you and me –

MOLLY: Sorry. Hang on. You haven't told anyone about the separation?

Pause.

STEPHEN: No.

MOLLY: No one? Since December –

STEPHEN: No.

MOLLY: God, Stephen. Why?

STEPHEN: Because…

Short pause.

STEPHEN: *(With great difficulty.)* I'm paralysed by the fuckin'
shame of it…

Short pause.

STEPHEN: This isn't America, Molly. It's Ireland. You've been
here, what, six, seven years now? You know what it's like.

MOLLY: Yeah, but, I mean, it's changing, the referendum –

STEPHEN: Ah referendum me hole. There was a referendum
in '86 – sixty-five per cent voted against divorce.

MOLLY: But that's nearly ten years ago.

STEPHEN: It doesn't fuckin' matter. It's not what you're
supposed to do. You get married. You stay married. "Til
death do us part.'

MOLLY: Yeah, well, you'll have to talk to your wife about that.

STEPHEN: No, that's not what I'm saying. I don't want to get
back with her. I fucked it up. And I've to live with that
now. I have to try and move on. Sort it out with Gerty. And
then maybe…you and me –

MOLLY: Fucking hell.

STEPHEN: Do you see what I'm saying –

MOLLY: Yes. I get it. I get it.

STEPHEN: Okay… Sorry.

Short pause.

MOLLY: Do you not think maybe your daughter ought to be
your priority here?

STEPHEN: She is. I just said that.

MOLLY: Well, sorry, maybe it's not my place to say, but I don't understand why you haven't seen her.

Silence. He's ashamed.

STEPHEN: It's complicated.

MOLLY: Oh c'mon, nothing is that complicated –

STEPHEN: Alright, Jesus. I wanted to see her. I didn't mean for this, for six months…

Short pause. She sighs audibly.

MOLLY: Fuck me. Welcome to the Hanrahan family.

Short pause.

MOLLY: Remember I said I imagined being in your house?

STEPHEN: What? Yeah –

MOLLY: This wasn't what I had in mind –

STEPHEN: Yeah, me either, okay. You don't need to fuckin' rub it in.

MOLLY: Okay.

Short pause.

STEPHEN: It's not funny.

MOLLY: I'm not laughing.

Pause.

MOLLY: *(Softer.)* What did you say her name is? Gerty?

STEPHEN: Yeah.

MOLLY: And she's how old?

STEPHEN: Eh…sixteen.

Short pause.

MOLLY: Is she a bit – I don't know, running away – is she a bit wild?

STEPHEN: No. No, she's, I mean, this, with her mother and me, you'd expect, wouldn't you?

MOLLY: Yeah, I suppose.

STEPHEN: Well, you would. No, she's eh, she's always been good, you know. Done well at school. Bit of a mouth on her sometimes, but no, she's a grand young one. You'd like her.

She smiles.

MOLLY: I'm sure she's lovely.

Short pause.

MOLLY: Although…Gerty…

Short pause.

STEPHEN: *(Not understanding her.)* Yeah?

MOLLY: Gertrude.

Short pause.

STEPHEN: I don't –

MOLLY: Not the best of omens, is it?

STEPHEN: Sorry?

MOLLY: Well, you know, Queen of Denmark. Bit of a bitch.

STEPHEN: Fuck off. Jesus.

Short pause.

STEPHEN: Her mother chose the name anyway.

MOLLY: Right, yeah. Not your fault.

STEPHEN: It's no one's fault. It's her name is all. There's nothing wrong with it.

MOLLY: No. Of course.

STEPHEN: Jesus Christ, what is the matter with you?

MOLLY: Sorry.

She smiles, pleased with herself.

Short pause.

MOLLY: It's Joyce as well, actually.

He's a step behind her, confused.

STEPHEN: Hah?

MOLLY: Gerty. She's one of the characters in *Ulysses.*

STEPHEN: *(Sarcastic.)* Really? Great –

MOLLY: *(With a gesture to illustrate.)* Bloom whacks one off on the beach in Sandymount while he's watching her.

STEPHEN: Ah look it, this is my daughter here. You can't be –

MOLLY: *(Half-laughing.)* Sorry.

STEPHEN: There's a line.

MOLLY: *(More sincere.)* No, I know. Sorry.

   Pause.

MOLLY: I was named after Molly Bloom.

STEPHEN: *(Sarcastic.)* Oh well done…I was named after an alcoholic fishmonger.

MOLLY: Uh…?

STEPHEN: My grandfather.

MOLLY: Oh.

STEPHEN: Yours is better.

   Short pause.

MOLLY: Stephen's in *Ulysses* too.

STEPHEN: Yeah.

MOLLY: He's a real prick.

STEPHEN: *(Quietly.)* God almighty…

   Short pause.

MOLLY: Sorry. You're not a prick. I know you're not…Look, I should probably go. Gerty could arrive early or –

STEPHEN: Yeah.

MOLLY: I'm sorry for…

STEPHEN: No, listen, it was my fault.

MOLLY: Well…

   Short pause.

MOLLY: I hope she's okay anyway. I really do.

There's an awkward moment when she considers kissing him or taking his hand but instead…

MOLLY: I'll uhm, you're not in 'til Monday, are you? I'll see you Monday.

Another awkward pause.

STEPHEN: Did we alleviate the terrible stench?

She smiles.

MOLLY: *(Gently.)* I think we made it worse, Stephen.

Short pause.

MOLLY: Bye.

She goes to leave.

STEPHEN: *(Sings.)* 'I shoulda known we'd never get far.'

She stops.

Short pause.

STEPHEN: The lyrics to that song can be applied to almost any situation.

She turns to face him.

MOLLY: I'm not saying that's it, okay? But just, this was a lot, you know, for one morning, so…

STEPHEN: Yeah.

Short pause.

STEPHEN: Me and Gerty used to listen to it when she was little.

Short pause.

MOLLY: What? *Summer of '69?*

STEPHEN: What are you making that face for?

MOLLY: Well, uh, it's not really appropriate, is it?

STEPHEN: Why not?

MOLLY: It's a celebration of a dirty sex act.

STEPHEN: Are you fuckin' mad? Are you actually fuckin' mad –

MOLLY: The 69.

STEPHEN: It's about nostalgia.

MOLLY: Nostalgia for a dirty sex act.

STEPHEN: *(Sings, as if to prove his point.)* 'Those were the best days of my life.'

MOLLY: *(Sings, contradicting him.)* 'Me and my baby *in a 69*'.

STEPHEN: It doesn't say that. It's 'Me and my baby in '69'.

MOLLY: Uh uh. 'Me and my baby in *a* 69'.

STEPHEN: I'll play it for you.

MOLLY: I'm going, Stephen. Bryan Adams even admitted it though.

STEPHEN: He did in his hole.

MOLLY: He did.

STEPHEN: Nope –

MOLLY: And no wonder she hasn't been to see you in six months if that's what you subjected her to as a child.

STEPHEN: Sorry. What?

MOLLY: I'm outta here –

STEPHEN: *(Light-hearted.)* Fuckin' right you are. Go on. Get.

He ushers her toward the door.

STEPHEN: *(As he goes, or off.)* You've gone too far now.

MOLLY: *(Mocking, as she goes, or off.)* Sorry.

They leave.

Lights out.

SCENE THREE

The same day, about half one in the afternoon. It's still raining.

The door opens.

STEPHEN: *(Off.)* Go on in.

GERTY walks in followed by STEPHEN, now fully dressed. She has a large plaster or bandage on her hand.

STEPHEN: Are you after getting wet?

GERTY: Nah, the umbrella sure –

STEPHEN: Right yeah…You got the DART out, did you?

GERTY: Ehm, yeah, well I had to get the bus first –

STEPHEN: Right…I can give you some of my clothes –

GERTY: I'm fine, dad. It's not that bad –

STEPHEN: Or there might be some of your own? Some tops or –

GERTY: Dad, I'm fine. Honestly. I didn't leave any clothes anyway…

STEPHEN: No.

Silence.

STEPHEN: Rain – that's the Irish affliction. God punishing us for being too perfect.

She smiles. Short pause.

STEPHEN: You look great.

GERTY: Do I?

STEPHEN: Yeah…No, you look a bit knackered actually.

GERTY: Didn't get much sleep.

STEPHEN: No.

Short pause.

GERTY: Mam says I'm looking more and more like you.

STEPHEN: Like me? Ah Jaysis, I hope not. You poor thing.

She smiles.

STEPHEN: No, if you had my looks sure you'd never get any rest. There'd be hordes of fellas chasing after you day and night –

GERTY: Dad.

STEPHEN: I'm only messing.

Short pause.

STEPHEN: I was a bit worried you'd show up looking like that Morticia Adams or one of them Cure-heads –

GERTY: Eh what?

STEPHEN: You know, with the make-up, and all the –

GERTY: A goth?

STEPHEN: *(Sensing her displeasure.)* Well, eh –

GERTY: *(Sarcastic.)* Yeah, dad. I'm a goth now. You wait there while I go cut myself in the jacks.

STEPHEN: *(Admonishing.)* Alright.

Short pause.

STEPHEN: *(Softer.)* Your tongue is sharp as ever.

Short pause.

STEPHEN: Your mother got some of it yesterday?

Silence.

STEPHEN: I spoke to her.

GERTY: Well done.

Short pause.

STEPHEN: You had a row.

GERTY: *(Sarcastic.)* Yep. Thought I'd keep it interesting, you know, 'cause we hadn't had one in ages.

Short pause.

STEPHEN: You're not getting on?

GERTY: What do you think?

Short pause.

STEPHEN: I'll have to call her.

GERTY: Don't, dad.

STEPHEN: She's worried, love.

GERTY: Please.

STEPHEN: I was worried too.

She sniggers or scoffs.

STEPHEN: What?

GERTY: You were worried, were you?

STEPHEN: Yes.

GERTY: Haven't forgotten me?

Silence.

STEPHEN: Is that what you think?

Silence.

GERTY: No.

Silence.

STEPHEN: I should've been in touch with you, love. I'm sorry –

GERTY: I need to tell you something, dad.

STEPHEN: I should call your mother.

GERTY: Are you listening?

STEPHEN: She came here –

GERTY: What?

STEPHEN: This morning. Looking for you.

GERTY: When?

STEPHEN: At like, eleven or something. If she finds out you're here and I've not contacted her…

She gives him a dirty look.

STEPHEN: I'll call her in a minute then, okay…Or she'll probably call herself. She's not expecting you here 'til two…

Silence.

STEPHEN: Did you get any lunch?

GERTY: I'm not hungry.

STEPHEN: Okay…

Short pause.

STEPHEN: I could do you a cup of tea?

GERTY: I don't drink tea. When did I ever drink tea?

STEPHEN: Yeah. Sorry…When do I ever have tea bags?

Short pause.

STEPHEN: How's eh, how's school?

GERTY: School's closed, dad. It's summer.

STEPHEN: Jays, this is going well, isn't it? Nice and relaxed.

She smiles in spite of herself.

STEPHEN: I know it's summer but, you know –

GERTY: School's okay. It's fine. I've not been expelled or suddenly started getting 'F's in all my subjects because my parents split up. Despite what Sister Burke says.

STEPHEN: What does Sister Burke say?

GERTY: Nothing. It doesn't matter… *(Softening.)* I meant to bring my report card, to show you but…

STEPHEN: That's alright. How'd eh, how did you do –

GERTY: Straight 'A's.

STEPHEN: Sure that's great.

GERTY: Except for Business Studies.

STEPHEN: Oh.

GERTY: And Maths.

STEPHEN: *(Smiles.)* That's not really straight 'A's then, is it?

GERTY: *(Smiles.)* No…Shut up.

STEPHEN: I'm only messing. You're doing great. Better than I ever did. I never got straight 'A's…Except for Business Studies and Maths.

GERTY: Stop it, would you? Stop making fun of me.

STEPHEN: I'm not. I'm serious. You *are* doing great.

Pause.

STEPHEN: I always thought Sister Burke was some sort of satanic underling.

She smiles.

STEPHEN: Rotten woman. Even by a nun's standards.

GERTY: She keeps going on at me about what happens to children from broken homes.

STEPHEN: What happens?

GERTY: We fail our Leaving.

STEPHEN: *(Sarcastic.)* Of course, yeah. Naturally.

GERTY: And become drug addicts and murderers. Or politicians.

STEPHEN: *(Appalled.)* She didn't say that.

GERTY: She did.

STEPHEN: The headmistress?

GERTY: Yes.

STEPHEN: Does your mother know?

GERTY: Too fuckin' right she does. They had a massive argument at the parent-teacher meeting.

STEPHEN: Good.

GERTY: No, it's not good. Sister Burke said she'd prefer it if I found another school, and she never would've let me in, in the first place, if she'd known…

Short pause.

STEPHEN: Known what?

GERTY: About you and mam, that your marriage was, you know…

STEPHEN: Ah, look it, she's a nun. She hasn't a fuckin' notion what marriage is like. Do you know what? Next time she says anything to you, if she even fuckin' looks at you crooked, ask her if there's any institution in the entire world more ignorant on the subject of marriage than the Catholic Church.

GERTY: *(Sarcastic.)* Yeah, I'll do that, dad. That's a great idea. She already hates me.

STEPHEN: Nuns hate everyone. That's why they become nuns.

GERTY: It's not just her anyway, is it?

STEPHEN: What do you mean?

GERTY: Nothing.

STEPHEN: Did someone else say something to you?

GERTY: No. I shouldn't've brought it up.

STEPHEN: Okay.

Silence.

That's a shocking thing to say to a child, though –

GERTY: Alright, dad.

STEPHEN: Well, it is…Sorry.

Silence.

STEPHEN: What are we gonna do about your mother?

GERTY: Just give it another few minutes, dad, please.

STEPHEN: I have to let her know, Gerty.

GERTY: There's something I need to tell you.

STEPHEN: You need to tell me where you were last night.

GERTY: For God's sake.

STEPHEN: Look, if she shows up and I can't explain to her –

GERTY: There's nothing to explain –

STEPHEN: Well, you must've stayed somewhere. Just tell me where it was.

GERTY: *(Sings, in a deep voice, Nirvana's version of 'Where did you sleep last night?'.)* 'My girl, my girl, don't lie to / me –' *(Continues.)*

STEPHEN: *(Overlapping.)* Ah Gerty –

GERTY: '– Tell me where did you sleep last night?'

STEPHEN: I'm serious.

GERTY: I went to a party, alright. It's no big deal.

STEPHEN: What party?

GERTY: A party. A friend's party.

STEPHEN: Your mother called all your friends, she said.

GERTY: She doesn't know all my friends.

STEPHEN: Could you not have called to let her know you were okay?

GERTY: I am okay.

STEPHEN: But your mother didn't know that. Could you not have called her –

GERTY: I got drunk, okay. I fell asleep.

STEPHEN: You got drunk?

GERTY: Yes.

Short pause.

STEPHEN: You're drinking?

GERTY: That's what I just said, isn't it?

STEPHEN: What're you drinking?

GERTY: Paint, what do you think?

STEPHEN: What're you drinking?

GERTY: Cider. Mostly cider.

STEPHEN: Where?

GERTY: Hah?

STEPHEN: Where do you go? To drink.

GERTY: Well, last night my friend's. But usually a field near the new house.

STEPHEN: A field?

GERTY: Yes. A field.

STEPHEN: Are there fellas there?

GERTY: *(Sarcastic.)* Yeah, IRA lads mainly. *(Sincere again.)* It's fine, dad. I have a flagon and roll around the grass like a

38

dandelion wish. *(Mocking, in an exaggerated Irish accent.)* The craic's only mighty, so it is.

STEPHEN: Does your mother know?

Silence.

STEPHEN: Does she?

GERTY: I don't know. It's no big deal anyway.

STEPHEN: 'Course it's a big deal. You're too young.

GERTY: My friends've all been drinking for years. Since they were twelve. I only just started. I should get some credit. An award or something. Soberest teenager in Ireland.

Short pause.

STEPHEN: You only started after –

GERTY: Yeah, dad. After my parents broke up. If you'd stayed together I woulda been a pioneer the whole rest of my life. And I would've cured cancer and AIDS and won the Olympics. But that's all gone now.

STEPHEN: *(Gently.)* Don't be such a smartalec. Are you taking drugs as well?

GERTY: Hmmm, let me see. Hash, speed, ecstasy – *(Continues.)*

STEPHEN: *(Overlapping.)* Ah stop it, would you?

GERTY: – coke, heroin, crystal meth, horse tranquilisers – *(Continues.)*

STEPHEN: *(Overlapping.)* I'm serious, Gerty.

GERTY: Poppers. Have you ever had poppers? They loosen the muscles in your ass.

STEPHEN: What? How do you know that?

GERTY: I'm not taking drugs, dad. I only follow your example.

STEPHEN: What's that supposed to mean?

GERTY: You were drunk half the time you were married, weren't you? I mean, I don't blame you. Probably the only way you could put up with her.

STEPHEN: Don't talk about your mother like that.

GERTY: Why not?

STEPHEN: Because.

GERTY: It's true, isn't it?

STEPHEN: I was no picnic to live with, Gerty. If anyone had a reason to get drunk, it was your mother. But she didn't. She was too busy looking after you. So cop yourself on, will you? She's a good woman and she cares about you. She's always done what's best for you. Show her some fuckin' respect.

Silence.

GERTY: I don't know why you're defending her. She says some nasty shit about you.

STEPHEN: Yeah, she has every right.

Short pause.

What nasty shit?

GERTY: Never mind.

STEPHEN: Nah, c'mon, what did she say?

GERTY: I'm not getting in the middle of it, Dad, okay. Not again.

STEPHEN: Okay.

Silence.

STEPHEN: I haven't had a drink in three months, by the way.

GERTY looks at the drinks cabinet or at the wine glass from last night.

STEPHEN: Until today. Until I found out you were missing.

GERTY: Jesus Christ. I'm not missing. Yer man from the *Manic Street Preachers* is missing. I'm not missing. I went to a fuckin' party.

STEPHEN: You should've told your mother where you were.

GERTY: You used to go missing yourself.

STEPHEN: *(Admonishing.)* Alright.

GERTY: We won't talk about that, will we not?

STEPHEN: There's a lot of things I'm not proud of. But that's not the issue right now, is it? We were both worried about you. We just want to know you're alright.

GERTY: Yeah, I'm fuckin' deadly, thanks. Never been better.

STEPHEN: There's a history of alcoholism in our family.

GERTY: *(Sarcastic.)* Really? I was not aware of that.

STEPHEN: I'm just saying. You need to be careful.

GERTY: Thanks for the advice. I'll bear it in mind.

STEPHEN: Your mother'll have a conniption if she finds out. Does she know already?

GERTY: You asked me that a minute ago.

STEPHEN: Is that what the row was about?

GERTY: No. I need to tell you something, dad.

STEPHEN: Right. I was listening to *Summer of '69* there –

GERTY: *(Baffled.)* What?

STEPHEN: *Summer of '69.*

GERTY: And?

STEPHEN: Do you not remember, we used to listen to it together when you were little?

GERTY: That filthy sex song?

STEPHEN: It's not a filthy sex song. It's about nostalgia.

GERTY: What the fuck – *what the actual fuck* – has that got to do with anything?

STEPHEN: I don't know. It's a song you used to like.

GERTY: Yeah and I used to like *My Little Pony.* Do you wanna talk about that too? I'm trying to tell you something.

STEPHEN: I don't know if I wanna hear it.

GERTY: *(Takes a second to realise.)* Aw, Jesus Christ, dad, I'm not pregnant, okay. My virginity is fully intact. You can relax.

Silence. He's visibly relieved.

STEPHEN: Alright…Go on then.

Short pause.

GERTY: Mam's moving to Cork.

Short pause.

STEPHEN: What do you mean?

GERTY: She's moving to Cork.

STEPHEN: To live?

GERTY: Yeah.

Short pause.

STEPHEN: Why?

Short pause.

GERTY: There's a man…

Silence.

STEPHEN: Who?

GERTY: I don't know. Noel is his name. He sells stationery.

Short pause.

STEPHEN: What, like, pencils?

GERTY: Yeah.

STEPHEN: She's moving to Cork for a man who sells pencils?

GERTY: Yes. She's gonna apply for a divorce as well, if the yoke passes, the referendum –

STEPHEN: Hang on, sorry –

GERTY: It's been going on for years, dad –

STEPHEN: Would you just give me a second?

Silence.

STEPHEN: Have you met him?

GERTY: Yes.

STEPHEN: Why are you fuckin' telling me this?

GERTY: Eh, you're her husband.

STEPHEN: Not anymore –

GERTY: Well, what about me? What am I supposed to do? My friends are here, dad. In Dublin. And school, I mean, obviously. I've only two years left. I can't just move. Especially given the, like, massive upheaval she's already put me through. Anyone would think she's actually trying to destroy my life. And what happens to us? If I move to Cork, when do we see each other…?

Silence.

GERTY: Yeah, exactly. I can't go. There's no fuckin' way.

Short pause.

STEPHEN: What're you suggesting then?

Pause.

GERTY: I was hoping maybe you'd let me stay here. With, with you.

STEPHEN: With me?

GERTY: Yes.

STEPHEN: Would you want that?

GERTY: Yes. Of course.

Short pause.

STEPHEN: *(A realisation.)* This was the row.

She nods.

STEPHEN: You said all this to her?

GERTY: I told her I'm not going.

STEPHEN: Right, but she wants you to, obviously?

GERTY: Anything to make sure I'm miserable.

STEPHEN: What did she say?

GERTY: She wouldn't even consider it. She said she'd made up her mind and that was it.

STEPHEN: Sounds like Marion, alright.

GERTY: But that's where you come in.

STEPHEN: Is it?

GERTY: Yes. You could always talk her 'round, dad. Whenever she got mad –

STEPHEN: I think this might be different, Gerty –

GERTY: Well, what then? You're just gonna let me fuckin' go?

STEPHEN: No, I'm not saying that. Would you calm down –

GERTY: Do you even want me to stay? Do you even care?

STEPHEN: Of course I care –

GERTY: Well then speak to her. Tell her I'm staying here with you.

STEPHEN: I can't just tell her. She's not going to accept that –

GERTY: You can try, can't you? That's the least you can do for me after six months of fuckin' nothing.

Silence.

GERTY: Sorry. I shouldn't've said that.

Silence.

GERTY: I'll just go if you want me to –

STEPHEN: I'll speak to her, Gerty.

Pause.

STEPHEN: We'll sort it out.

GERTY: Thank you. Sorry.

STEPHEN: You've nothing to be sorry for. I –

GERTY: Dad –

An awkward pause.

GERTY: Just –

Another awkward pause before she goes to hug him, but he instinctively moves away and the moment is gone.

STEPHEN: I'll call her now.

GERTY: Okay. Eh, I might go up and have a kip until she gets here.

STEPHEN: Alright. Your room is still… *(He's about to say 'there' but he realises how obvious this is.).* Yeah, I'll see you in a little while.

She nods, then goes to leave.

STEPHEN: Gerty.

She turns to face him.

GERTY: Yeah?

Pause.

STEPHEN: Pencils?

GERTY: Yeah.

Pause.

STEPHEN: What's he like?

She shrugs.

GERTY: I don't know. Ugly. He's got a moustache.

STEPHEN: Really?

GERTY: Yeah. Big long fuckin' thing. Like one of those hoover attachments, do you know, with the bristles.

STEPHEN: Jesus, yeah.

Pause.

STEPHEN: If you picked him up, could you *(He pretends to pick up, and hoover with, an imaginary Noel.)* –

She laughs.

GERTY: Dad –

He directs the imaginary hoover at her, pretends to hoover her.

GERTY: *(Laughing.)* Stop it.

He breaks off for a second to say –

STEPHEN: Hoover face.

Immediately, then, he resumes the hoover attack on her, but very quickly she says –

GERTY: Actually, dad, this is kind of disgusting.

He stops.

STEPHEN: What? Oh. Yeah.

GERTY: I don't really want him to –

STEPHEN: No. Sorry. I didn't mean to –

GERTY: No, I know, just…

Short pause.

GERTY: I hope I don't think of that now, every time I see him.

STEPHEN: No. Sorry.

He suddenly makes a hoover noise again.

GERTY: Dad –

He stops again.

STEPHEN: Sorry.

GERTY: It's not funny.

STEPHEN: Won't happen again.

GERTY: Jesus.

STEPHEN: Promise. I promise.

Short pause.

GERTY: Anyway, eh –

STEPHEN: Yeah, you go on up, and I'll call Marion.

GERTY: Okay.

She lingers awkwardly for a short time, then goes out. He pauses for a moment, deep in thought, then goes to the drinks cabinet for more whiskey.

Lights out.

SCENE FOUR

About an hour or so later the same day. Still no sign of the rain abating.

The door opens, and MARION powers into the room, followed by STEPHEN.

MARION: No way. No fuckin' way.

STEPHEN: Why not?

MARION: Not a chance.

STEPHEN: She doesn't want to go, Marion.

MARION: That's neither here nor there.

STEPHEN: Of course, it is –

MARION: Look, can I just go up and wake her?

STEPHEN: She wants to stay with me, she said. She told me.

MARION: So the fuck what? That obviously can't happen.

STEPHEN: What do you mean 'obviously'? Why is it so obvious?

MARION: Ah c'mon, Stephen, would you get serious?

STEPHEN: I *am* serious.

MARION: She can't stay with you.

STEPHEN: Why?

MARION: Are you fuckin' mad? Sure, who'd be looking after who?

STEPHEN: What's that supposed to mean?

MARION: You work it out.

STEPHEN: She told me you'll be looking for a divorce.

MARION stops. Short pause.

STEPHEN: If it, if the thing passes.

Silence.

MARION: That's hardly a surprise, is it?

STEPHEN: I suppose not –

MARION: Here's one vote the 'yes' camp can rely on.

STEPHEN: *(Sarcastic.)* Oh, I'm sure they're delighted.

Short pause.

STEPHEN: You'll have to wait four years, you know? That's how long it says, the legislation – the couple have to have lived apart for four of the last five years.

MARION: So I'll wait.

    Silence.

STEPHEN: Nigel – is that his name?

MARION: Don't start this.

STEPHEN: Start what? *(Playing with the name.)* Nigel –

MARION: It's Noel. You know it is –

STEPHEN: Noel. Sorry.

MARION: *('No, you're not'.)* Yeah.

STEPHEN: Sells stationery.

MARION: That's right.

STEPHEN: Very masculine job, that. Does he have a shatterproof ruler?

MARION: What about your little friend from this morning? What was her name?

STEPHEN: *(Taken aback.)* I don't think that's relevant –

MARION: The young one from the Christmas party last year, wasn't it? What was her name again? Eh –

STEPHEN: None of your business.

MARION: Molly, was it?

STEPHEN: Eh –

MARION: Like Molly Malone. The dirty fish-smelling prostitute.

STEPHEN: Oh, you're fuckin' gas, Marion. She was named after Molly Bloom, actually.

MARION: Is that right? Sure, she was a prostitute as well. I see what you're trying to do, Stephen, but just so we're clear, I feel no guilt whatsoever. None.

STEPHEN: I'm not asking you to –

    They notice GERTY standing in the doorway.

GERTY: Why're you talking about prostitutes?

MARION: C'm'ere to me, you.

She hugs GERTY.

MARION: Thank God you're safe.

She hugs her again.

MARION: I could murder you, do you know that? Do you have any idea the worry you put me through?

GERTY: Sorry.

MARION: Let me have a look at you –

STEPHEN: Did we wake you, love? Sorry.

GERTY: No. It's okay. I couldn't sleep anyway. The rain.

MARION: *(Referring to the bandage on GERTY's hand.)* What's that?

GERTY: What?

MARION: That. On your hand. What happened to you?

GERTY: Nothing.

MARION: It's not nothing. Look it. Did you see this, Stephen?

STEPHEN: Eh, no –

MARION: You told me she was alright. Exhibit A. Did you not even ask her –

GERTY: It's nothing, mam. I just, I cut myself. It was an accident.

MARION: Show me your hand, please.

GERTY: I said it's nothing.

MARION: Gerty, show me your hand.

STEPHEN: Show her, love.

GERTY: For fuck's sake –

MARION: Don't you fuckin' curse at your father, young lady.

GERTY: I wasn't cursing *at* him, was I –

STEPHEN: Alright the pair of you. Can we just have a look at your hand here please?

GERTY: Oh, it's 'we' now, is it? All of a sudden.

STEPHEN: What? No. Just –

MARION: Gerty, if something has happened to you, I need to know –

GERTY: Nothing's happened.

MARION: Show me your hand then.

STEPHEN: Go on, Gerty. Please.

GERTY: It's just a little nick. Jesus. You don't need to get all Gestapo about it.

Pause. They both look at her.

GERTY: Alright. God. *(Offering her hand to MARION.)* Here. Be careful.

MARION: I will.

MARION carefully removes the plaster.

GERTY: Ow. Watch it.

MARION recoils in shock when she sees GERTY's hand.

MARION: Oh my / God –

GERTY: Mam, it's not –

STEPHEN: What? Show me…

He looks at GERTY's hand.

STEPHEN: Mother of fuck –

MARION: Who did this to you?

GERTY: No one.

MARION: I want to know who did this to you.

STEPHEN: What is it?

MARION: Cigarette burns.

STEPHEN: What?

GERTY: No it's not. I cut myself. That's all.

MARION: Gerty, I'm not stupid. Do you think in my line of work –

STEPHEN: Did someone burn you?

GERTY: No. It was…I had an accident. I was cutting some bread.

MARION: Where were you last night?

GERTY: I already told dad. I was at a party.

MARION: I don't believe you.

GERTY: It's true.

MARION: Where then? What party?

GERTY: At a friend's. I told dad.

MARION: What friend's?

GERTY: You don't know them.

MARION: Well, do they have a name? Can you tell me where they live? 'Cause I need to talk to their parents.

GERTY: Mam –

STEPHEN: Marion, I don't think that's going to help.

MARION: Stephen, shut the fuck up. Leave this to me –

GERTY: Don't talk to dad like that –

STEPHEN: *(To MARION.)* I'm trying to help –

MARION: Well, you're not, so just fuckin' –

STEPHEN: Right so, fuck ye then.

They watch as he goes to the drinks cabinet and starts to make himself a drink.

MARION: Are you fuckin' having me on?

STEPHEN: What?

MARION: What do you think you're doing?

STEPHEN: Meditating, Marion. What does it look like?

MARION: Can you not deal with anything without…Your daughter's been injured – *(Continues.)*

GERTY: *(Overlapping.)* I'm not injured –

MARION: – and your solution, as usual, as per the fuckin' norm, is to get drunk.

STEPHEN: I am not getting drunk. I'm having a drink. There's a difference. And I'll do whatever the fuck I like in my own house.

MARION: Yeah, regardless of anyone else, your daughter or –

STEPHEN: I was trying to fuckin' help. You told me / to *(Unsaid: 'stay out of it'.)* –

GERTY: *(Raises her voice.)* Okay. Alright. I was drunk.

Short pause.

GERTY: *(Lowers her voice again.)* I was drinking. We all were… We were hammered. And, I don't know, we just, we started messing.

MARION: Messing. What does *(Unsaid: 'that mean?'.)* –

GERTY: Playing a game.

MARION: A game?

GERTY: Yes. Just, like, burning each other. With the…For a laugh, like –

MARION: You were burning each other with cigarettes? For a laugh?

GERTY: Yes. You can hardly feel it when you're pissed.

MARION: God almighty, how drunk were you?

Silence.

MARION: Why would you…Why would anyone –

GERTY: To see how long you can last.

MARION: Last what?

GERTY: The pain. How long you can take the pain.

MARION: Jesus, Mary and Joseph –

GERTY: I'm sorry, okay.

MARION: Why would you –

GERTY: I won't do it again.

MARION: I don't understand –

GERTY: Look, I'm not gonna have you guilt-tripping me when you've been fuckin' someone behind dad's back.

STEPHEN: Gerty, that's not – You can't say that.

GERTY: Why not? It's true, isn't it?

Silence.

MARION: *(To STEPHEN.)* Get me one, would you?

He looks at her, baffled.

STEPHEN: Eh?

MARION: A drink.

Short pause.

STEPHEN: But you –

MARION: Just get me a fuckin' drink, Stephen, for Christ's sake.

STEPHEN: Alright. Jesus fuck.

He goes to the drinks cabinet.

STEPHEN: *(To himself.)* At least men are consistent. *(To MARION.)* Whiskey?

MARION: *('Whatever'.)* Yes.

He pours her a drink, brings her the glass. She downs it in one as he and GERTY watch, stunned. MARION gives the glass back to him.

MARION: We should get going, Stephen.

GERTY: I'm not leaving.

MARION: *(To GERTY.)* We'll discuss this *(Meaning her hand.)* at home –

GERTY: This is my home –

MARION: I'm sorry, Gerty, but it's not anymore –

GERTY: Yes, it is. I'm staying here –

MARION: No, you're not –

GERTY: Are you deaf or something? Can you not hear me? I'm not going with you. I'm not going to Cork –

STEPHEN: Gerty, will you calm down? Listen, Marion, maybe it's better if she stays here for now.

GERTY: I'm staying here forever.

MARION: No, you're not.

GERTY: You can't stop me.

MARION: I can and I will.

STEPHEN: One night, Marion. That's all. Until we sort this out.

GERTY: It is sorted. I'm staying here.

MARION: You're not.

GERTY: I am.

MARION: *(Shouts.)* Why are you doing this to me, hah? Is it not enough you had me up all night worrying –

GERTY: That was your own fuckin' fault –

MARION: What?

STEPHEN: Will the pair of you stop?

GERTY: It was your own fuckin' fault. You made me run off. You're driving me away. Just like you drove dad away.

STEPHEN: *(Overlapping.)* Oh Jaysis –

He goes for another drink.

MARION: *(Overlapping, to GERTY, really exploding.)* Are you fuckin' serious? You think I drove your father away? You think I wanted this? Do you? My family fallen to shreds. You treating me like I'm less than dirt. Your granny on the phone to me every chance she gets, letting me know in the nicest possible way how ashamed she is of me, and that, that *(As though the word is an insult.)* nun from the school – *(Continues.)*

STEPHEN: *(Overlapping.)* Ah now look –

MARION: – that fuckin' *nun* telling me my child is going to hell unless I go back to my husband –

STEPHEN: You can't be listening to that oul' wagon –

MARION: Well someone has to listen to her, Stephen. Someone has to deal with her. Someone has to drop Gerty to school. And go to the meetings. And pick her up from her hockey. But you wouldn't know that, would you? 'Cause you're not around.

STEPHEN: Look, that's not – I apologised to Gerty for that –

MARION: Oh great, Stephen. Dad of the year 1995. I'm very happy for you. Tell you what, I'll raise our daughter, will I? And you can offer her an apology every six months.

STEPHEN: I'm saying she can live with me. What more do you want? She can stay with me while you swan off to Cork with pencil-dick –

MARION: I am not swanning off anywhere. The fuckin' nerve of you. How many times did you go missing, hah?

GERTY: Okay, if you're just gonna shout at each other, like a pair of children, I'm going.

MARION: Gerty, hang on. I know you're angry with me. You've every right to be. I've made mistakes. I know I have. And I'm sorry. I am. But it wasn't just me. You need to understand that. Your father played his part, my God.

STEPHEN: This is not the issue, Marion.

MARION: Of course it's the issue. Why should I take all the blame? I've had six months of it and I'm sick and fuckin' tired. Somehow I've ended up the villain here –

GERTY: Uh, yeah, because you betrayed your husband.

MARION: Oh, the saint, yes. How stupid of me? I betrayed Saint Stephen Hanrahan. A stranger to alcohol and women and lies –

STEPHEN: *(Raises his voice.)* That's enough.

MARION: No, it fuckin' isn't, Stephen. It isn't. And I don't think the young one I found half-naked beneath you – *(Continues.)*

STEPHEN: *(Overlapping, really exploding.)* Enough –

MARION: – this morning would think it's enough either –

STEPHEN: Jesus Christ, Marion. I said enough. Look, she doesn't want to go with you. You need to face up to that.

MARION: Yeah. Always been a bit slow on the uptake though, haven't I? Always been a woman to overlook what was staring right fuckin' at me –

STEPHEN: I'm warning you, Marion –

MARION: Took me eighteen years to realise I couldn't change a philandering drunk into a decent, honourable man – *(Continues.)*

GERTY: *(Overlapping, quietly.)* What young one?

MARION: – but now, you see, I've actually found someone decent and honourable. Do you think I'm going to let go of that?

GERTY: *(Louder.)* What young one?

STEPHEN: Gerty, listen –

MARION: What young one, Stephen?

STEPHEN: This is not the issue –

GERTY: Was someone here earlier?

STEPHEN: No –

MARION: No, there wasn't, Gerty. No. I imagined it. Just like I imagined him not picking up the phone last night while he fucked her –

GERTY: What?

STEPHEN: Jesus –

MARION: Just like I imagined what he did with her last year –

STEPHEN: Marion –

MARION: Just like I imagined all the others –

STEPHEN: This is shameful –

GERTY: What others?

MARION: Are you joking? Do you not know –

STEPHEN: Don't listen to her, Gerty. She's manipulating you. *(To MARION.)* Shameful. Fuckin' shameful.

MARION: *(Exploding.)* Will I tell you what shame is, will I? Shame is when your three-year-old daughter comes into you first thing in the morning and asks where her daddy is and you have to lie to her 'cause you don't fuckin' know. That's shame, Stephen.

STEPHEN: You better shut the fuck up, Marion –

GERTY: Dad –

MARION: Shame is when the man you married arrives home in the middle of the night so drunk he climbs up on top of you in the bed and pisses in your face –

STEPHEN: *(Really exploding.)* Just shut your fuckin' mouth. You say one more fuckin' thing –

He pushes her down onto the couch.

Pause. Everything freezes until –

GERTY: Mam –

MARION gets up, goes to GERTY.

STEPHEN: Get out. Go on. The pair of you.

GERTY: What?

STEPHEN: *(In GERTY's face.)* Fuck off.

GERTY: Dad, what're you doing?

STEPHEN: Get the fuck out of my house. I don't want you here.

MARION: *(To GERTY.)* C'mon Gerty.

STEPHEN: Get out.

MARION: C'mon.

GERTY: Dad.

STEPHEN: Out. Go. Just fuckin' go.

MARION: *(To GERTY.)* Gerty, please.

GERTY: *(Feeble, as MARION escorts her off.)* I don't understand…
(A plea.) Dad –

STEPHEN: *(Roars.)* Get out.

GERTY: I don't understand…

MARION and GERTY leave. STEPHEN is left alone, still enraged.

STEPHEN: *(Hurls books from one of the shelves.)* Fuck.

Lights out.

SCENE FIVE

The following day, about noon. The rain has stopped. Sunlight is creeping in through the window. STEPHEN is sitting on the couch in the same clothes as yesterday. It appears he has been here all night. The whiskey bottle is now empty on the floor.

There's a knock on the front door of the house, off. He hears it but doesn't move.

A louder knock.

STEPHEN: *(Getting up.)* Alright. Would you…Jaysis.

He goes out. We hear the front door opening, muffled voices, the door closing.

He returns followed by MOLLY.

MOLLY: Sorry, I've got to go in to the office. *(Sees the books on the floor.)* I uh…I wanted to…I thought I'd just come and see how you're doing first.

Silence.

MOLLY: How was… Your daughter, did she –

STEPHEN: Yes.

MOLLY: Did it…Is she okay?

STEPHEN: Yes.

MOLLY: And the two of you –

STEPHEN: It went well, yeah. All sorted.

MOLLY: Oh, that's good. I'm glad to hear that.

Silence.

MOLLY: Are you okay?

STEPHEN: Yes.

MOLLY: You seem a bit –

STEPHEN: I'm fine. You don't need to worry about me.

MOLLY: Okay. Good.

Silence.

MOLLY: I'm fine too. Thanks for asking.

STEPHEN: You're welcome.

Silence.

MOLLY: This is… I uh… I wanted to talk about…about some of the things we…from yesterday –

STEPHEN: Yeah.

Silence.

MOLLY: Uhm, okay.

Short pause.

MOLLY: I'm taking the job, Stephen. But I don't think I can be with you.

STEPHEN: Right.

MOLLY: I don't think I can trust you. I'm sorry if that's, if it's harsh, but that's, I have to be honest with you. And, and honest with myself. I need to be with someone who makes me feel…who I can trust one hundred per cent and I don't… I don't think you can give that to me…

Short pause.

MOLLY: 'Cause I've been hurt before, you see, and… In any case I don't know if you're *(Perhaps unsaid: 'ready'.)* … I'm sorry.

Silence.

MOLLY: Is that –

STEPHEN: I understand what you're saying.

MOLLY: *(A little surprised.)* You do?

STEPHEN: Yes.

MOLLY: Okay…Good.

Silence.

MOLLY: Do you think, I mean…Do you think it'll be a problem then, us working together?

STEPHEN: No. I'll just get them to withdraw the offer.

MOLLY: What?

STEPHEN: I'll get them to withdraw the offer. I'll tell the *Times* I changed my mind. I made a mistake. You're not good enough. Whatever…

MOLLY: You can't do that.

STEPHEN: I can.

MOLLY: You wouldn't, Stephen.

STEPHEN: Really, you being offered the job was *entirely* down to me. I can just undo it. No big deal.

MOLLY: Jesus Christ.

STEPHEN: I only asked them to give it to you in the first place 'cause I wanted to fuck you.

He goes to the drinks cabinet, picks up a bottle of vodka.

STEPHEN: You're not even that good a reporter.

MOLLY: *(Stunned.)* How can you…?

Short pause.

MOLLY: *(Feeble.)* You fucking bastard.

He turns to her. She slaps him across the face.

He opens the bottle of vodka, tosses the cap aside, drinks.

She swings at him again. He catches her by the arm.

MOLLY: What are you…Stephen.

They struggle a moment, then he forces her backward, pours the vodka on to her head, pushes her down on to the floor, stands over her with the empty bottle raised, ready to hit her with it. She's crying, screaming.

STEPHEN: You're not so fuckin'…Now hah…Are you? Are you?

He stands over her a moment longer, then turns away. She stays on the floor, shocked, in tears.

STEPHEN: *(Unable to look at her.)* I'm sorry.

She still hasn't moved. She weeps quietly.

STEPHEN: I won't tell the *Times* to withdraw the offer. I didn't mean any of that, anything I said.

He turns to her, moves toward her. She squeals in fright. He bends down to her.

STEPHEN: I'm just a twisted oul' bollocks. I'm sorry. I'm just a twisted oul' bollocks.

He's on his knees now in front of her, his head on the floor.

After a moment, she rises unsteadily to her feet, goes to the door, leaves. We hear her going out, the sound of the front door opening and closing, off.

He is alone, on the floor, angry, in tears. Eventually he gets up, goes to the window, stands, looks out. The sunlight seems to stream in brighter and brighter.

Lights out.

End.

www.ingramcontent.com/pod-product-compliance
Ingram Content Group UK Ltd.
Pitfield, Milton Keynes, MK11 3LW, UK
UKHW020710030325
455689UK00009BA/180